BATS, BATS, BATS!

Building the Bat House

BATS, BATS, BATS!
Building the Bat House

Brad Spacone

JoHazel Publishing
Land O Lakes, Florida 34639

Published by: JoHazel Publishing
Land O Lakes, Florida 34639

ISBN: 978-0-9975645-1-8

Cover design © by C. C. Taylor
Interior photos and sketches furnished by Brad Spacone
Printed in United States

First Edition

Publisher's Email for permissions:

publisher@johazelpublishing.com
In the subject write: permission or bulk order request oordinator

Special bulk order prices available for purchases of 25 books or more. Please contact the publisher for rates at the above email . Please put in subject line: Bulk order price request

Acknowledgements

I would like to thank my neighbor and publisher, Chris Coad Taylor, for the opportunity to raise awareness of the role bats play in the environment.

Most praise is reserved for my persevering wife, Debbie, for transcribing and the photography. The older I get, the more I appreciate what a great mate she is to me.

Welcome to the fascinating world of

Bats, Bats, Bats!

Assets to the Environment:

Bats are mammals and make up about 25% of the mammal population. They are very well camouflaged so you really don't know how many there are.

An average bat will consume 3,000 – 5,000 insects per night, depending on the type of bat and its size.

What is the Book About?

If you have ever thought about building a bat house or wanted to, then this book will show you how easy it is to do. You will find answers to all your questions and step-by-step instructions, plus interesting facts that will surprise you about the misunderstood bat.

Inside you will get:

- Dimensions for the bat house.
- A supply list.
- How to attract the bats.
- And much, much more.

In the Beginning

Hi, my given name is Bradley, which is what my mother would yell when she was mad. Brad is the shortened name for a guy in his 50s, unless his wife is mad at him, then I am Bradley again! My life story begins in Tampa, Florida as a second-generation native. If you have never been to Florida, DO NOT come in the middle of summer. It is hot, humid, and extremely buggy. Yes, I said buggy. Buggy, that is, with mosquitoes and other small flying insects! This is because of all the summer rains we have in Florida; it makes for good insect breeding. But more on that subject later.

I am 52 and married to a lovely woman named Deb, who supports me in any project I start. And boy, have I started a few! I also have a daughter, Katrina (who is expecting her first baby) and a son, Vinny. Deb and I got married back (way back) in 1985 and lived in Tampa. We actually lived in the house I grew up in. In 2000, we moved to Land O Lakes. Did I forget to mention where I work? I am a telephone technician for the local phone company.

I am a do-it-yourself kind of guy and I come from a do-it-yourself family. I would rather build it or fix it myself if I can. I have built a concrete workshop (with the help of my dad), poured a concrete driveway (again with the help of my dad and brother), built my own solar panels to heat my pool, made my wife a scrapbooking cabinet, and converted an existing entertainment center to fit a larger TV.

I made bookcases for the kid's rooms and took my old baby crib, updated it for my own kids, and just this year, I redid the whole thing again so my daughter Katrina and her husband Justin can use it for their new baby.

Oh, and the neighbors call me a monkey because I would rather climb a tree and cut branches than hire someone. I've had dirt brought in to fill in low spots and re-sodded my grass myself with the help of the family (much to their dismay). No project is too big, you just have to think about it a little longer!

Why Build a Bat House?

As I said, we lived in Tampa before moving to Land O Lakes. We actually lived in the house I grew up in. Did I mention that this house butted up to a huge apartment complex? As the years went by, the tenants' quality diminished and the noise level went up. Robert Frost said "fences make good neighbors," but fences don't control excessive noise.

In 1999, we decided it was time for a change and we decided to move. My wife went out as a scout, to look at potential homes from the newspaper ads during the week. One weekend in March of 2000 I found a house for sale by owner in the paper in (drum roll) Land O Lakes. I didn't know much about Land O Lakes, but I did like the name.

That day, Debbie went out and looked at it. She wouldn't say much about the area or the house, all she would say is she didn't want me to be influenced by her thoughts of it. A few evenings later, we drove out to this property I now call home. It was just over 2000 square feet on .75 acre on a cul-de-sac. It also had a stagnant canal in the rear and cypress heads. This property was off the main drag, so it had little traffic, and no city lights. I started to understand why Deb would not give me her opinion of the area or house. We could actually see the stars! We were going to be living in paradise!

Since the current owner also had children in school, we decided to buy the property and rent it back to them until the end of the school year. I had to wait to live in my slice of heaven.

In June, we moved in. Moving is a perfect time to find out how many true friends you have. It was a hectic time, with back breaking work. At my old house, my father and I had built a 12 X 20 workshop. For the new house, my father purchased me a 12 X 20 utility shed as a present. I had it installed to the rear of the property near the canal and cypress head to be out of sight. I bring this up because remember, I am a DYI kind of guy and like to do projects in this aforementioned shop. All the stars were aligned, I thought. A beautiful home, a preserve at the rear, and good neighbors.

It did not take us too long to realize that paradise had a big problem. At dusk the mosquitoes would eat you alive! If you wanted to go outside after dark—forget it. The buzzing, the biting, the slapping, you get the picture. I found out after covering yourself with lots of repellant you could get by. This is if you didn't mind the irritation on your skin. And so, this is how we had to operate in the summer.

My son Vinny had become friends with a boy in the neighborhood and Deb and I then became friends with the parents. These next-door neighbor friends knew that I worked for a phone company and asked if I could get him some telephone poles. I wondered why so I asked, "What would you need poles for?" Seems his daughter had a school project of building a bat house and had a template for building it. He thought that after building the project with his daughter he didn't want to just store or throw away the houses.

Thus, he wanted to use them but needed a tall pole to attach it to . . . a telephone pole came to mind and then he remembered me! The neighbor said the bats were good for eating insects and mosquitoes. A natural way of fighting and controlling these pesky bugs. And so, it was on! A new project that I hoped would have long-term effects for my family.

Single Chamber House:

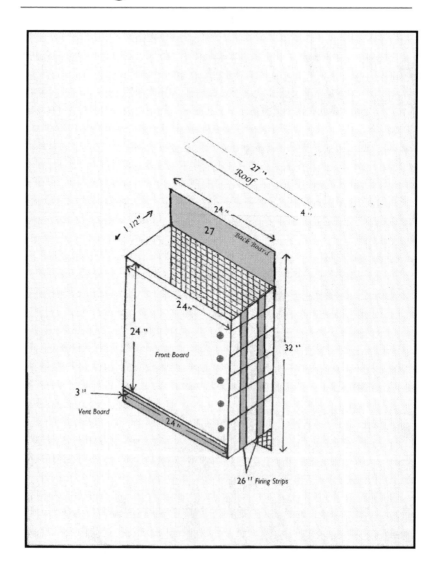

Building Materials Needed (for a single chamber house):

- 4 foot x 8 foot ½" pressure treated plywood
- Latex caulk
- Galvanized drywall screws
- Pressure treated furring strips
- Primer
- Oil-based paint
- Metal screen cloth
- 15-18 foot pole (a telephone pole or a pressure treated 4X4 will work)
- (2) 2" lag bolts with washers
- 3" utility brush

The materials and quantities listed under items needed are for a single chamber bat house. You can build more chambers (houses) out from main pole but this is heavier and more cumbersome to install. Additionally, double chamber style houses are harder to maintain.

I have two poles with a single chamber/house on both sides of each pole, for a total of four houses.

Step-by-Step Instructions

- Cut your backboard 24" wide X 32" high. This is the back plate you will be attaching to the pole.
- Next, cut your front plate 24" X 24" and set aside for now.
- Cut (4) furring strips 26" long.

- With a pair of metal side cutters, cut a screen 23 ¾" wide by 29" long. Starting from what will be the bottom staple screen toward top. The staples are to temporarily hold the screen in place before attaching furring strips. The width is slightly narrower than 24" because you don't want the metal exposed.

- Drop down 3" from what will be the top and double stack 2 furring strips (one on top of another) to each side. You will be sandwiching the screen between backboard and the first furring strip.

Pre-drill furring strips with enough spacing for 5 coarse threaded screws. These can be alternately installed from the backside, as well as the front. (Drywall screws work great.)

Note: By adding the furring strips over the screen, you are tightening the screen up.

- At this point, you have 2 furring strips double stacked on the backboard to hold down the screen.
- Dropping down on the backboard 3" from the top where the furring strips start, place top piece of plywood.
- Pre-drill and attach 5 screws to each side.
- For the roof, cut a piece of the plywood 4" X 27". This will be placed at a slight forward angle and screwed into the top of the furring strips. This large size and angle will allow for water run-off.

The picture above shows house with attached plywood cover with screen.

Drop down approximately 1" from the top cover and attach to protruding furring strips. Pre-drill these holes, also. (This drop-down piece will allow airflow as this house could hold over 100 bats during a hot summer.)

Note: Do not make this opening too large as predators could get inside.

- Next step is to apply latex caulk on all exterior seams where water could penetrate. Also, cover any exposed screw heads, as this makes a smoother-looking house front.
  - Cover the sides between furring strips, the roof, and plywood edges.
  - Paint exterior with a paint primer. Let primer thoroughly dry. Apply two coats of an oil based semi-gloss paint using a light color. Appling two coats will add durability.

Note: Let caulk thoroughly dry. The first house I built, I used a dark color to hide mildew and the heat inside the house caused the bats to hang outside on the landing screen. This left them open to birds of prey. I repainted with an off-white color, which lowered the inside temperature and solved the problem.

  - Pre-drill one hole at the top and one hole at the bottom in the center for attaching to the pole.

You can now attach the bat house to the pole with galvanized lag bolts and washers. Be sure to use caulk around these holes, also. If pole has not been set in the ground, you can attach the house while on the ground. If the pole is already set in the ground, then you will need to muscle the house up with you on a ladder and attach. I would suggest attaching the house to the pole before setting it in the ground.

The Bats' Humble Abode

Setting the Mounting Pole:

HELPFUL HINT: Before setting the pole in the ground, I suggest you have (but not required) a posthole digger and a piece of scrap board or plywood 6" wide x 4 feet long.

Dig a hole 3 ft. deep with posthole digger. Place board in hole vertically. Put end of pole over hole touching wood. If you can find four strong young men with work gloves, place the tallest man at the farthest end of the pole. Have all the men lift the pole and work slowly up. The board in the hole will guide the pole down into the hole. Fill dirt around the pole, tamping down as you fill to stabilize the pole further.

- Set the pole in the ground a minimum of 3 feet deep for safety, as bat houses will catch the wind. There have been many beautiful houses that were mounted way too low. Bats drop out of the houses in full flight and need ample room between house and ground.

- Next step is to sit and wait. Don't get discouraged, as it took me over one year to attract them. The last step after finally having bats move in is to start enjoying the great outdoors!

In the photo above, are two single-chamber houses that are home for over 200 Brazilian Free-tailed bats.

Maintenance

After so many hot Florida summers, I noticed that the paint would eventually begin to peel off the exterior. Therefore, you will have some painting maintenance to do every few years to avoid wood rot and decay.

During the winter months, when the temperature drops close to freezing, the bats may leave the houses for a few days until it warms up. This is an excellent time get an extension ladder (or you can use binoculars) to inspect the structure of your bat houses for routine maintenance.

If maintenance is needed, remove any paint that is loose with a scraper or putty knife.

Using a mild detergent and a scrub brush, clean the house thoroughly, making sure to get rid of any mold or mildew.

Rinse with fresh, clean water and let dry. After the house has thoroughly dried, inspect it for any loose caulk at the seams that has cracked, and replace as needed.

After caulk has completely dried, repaint with semi-gloss, light-colored exterior oil based paint.

The oil-based paint seems to last longer for me, versus the latex.

Periodically inspect the pole the houses are hanging on for rot. Other than these steps of maintenance, there isn't much else that needs to be done.

Just enjoy watching nature at its best.

Bats, Bats, Bats
How to Build a Bats House

Height of a bat house is extremely important. Too low, you will not get any move-ins.

Photos taken at
Lake Rogers Park

Do and Don'ts for Bat Houses:

Do put in a somewhat open area away from trees and house. They will need this open area for the drop off out from the house and lift up to fly away. Above the ground at least 12' or higher.

Do put a piece of metal over the top of the pole for further protection from the elements. It's just another way to prolong the life of your bat house. The metal just needs to be big enough to cover the pole. (I've used the heavier pie plates from frozen pies from the grocery store. Put a nail through the center and silicone around it for weather durability.)

Remember when I said that I lived in Land O Lakes, Florida? The key word here is *lakes*, there is plenty of water. A friend at work built some bat houses just north of me, thirty minutes away. He had a full house until he moved his above-ground swimming pool. No water source for the bats, means no bats. He needed to replace the water source with something else. And his wife suggested an inflatable kiddie pool. A short time afterward, the bats returned to roost.

Do NOT make your bat house entrance too large. This may allow predators to invade, allowing for easy pickings.

INTERESTING SIDE NOTE:

Since bats feed off of insects or fruit, the bat guano that falls around your post pole is very rich in Nitrogen, Phosphorus, and Potassium. The guano can be used fresh or dried as plant food.

Only a small amount is needed due to the high Nitrogen level for faster green growth and overall plant health and has little or no odor. Work into the soil before planting to help enrich the soil and improve drainage. It also acts as a natural fungicide and help control nematodes.

RECIPE FOR PLANT FOOD MIXTURE:

Mix 1 cup of guano to 1 gallon of water. Let sit overnight, and then spray on leaves. Use within one day of mixing.

Additional valued use: Adding guano to your compost will help speed up the decomposition process.

The Mosquito Conditions
in my Yard Now

Having bats has not eradicated all the mosquitos from my yard. Outside influences such as standing water still breed them. However, the issue has improved about 90%.

My close neighbors have remarked about the lessening of the mosquitos and other small bothersome insects.

All in all, the hardest part of the whole process of the bat house is the pole. You have to have a pole over 15 feet tall, preferably one 18 feet tall.

Getting the pole may be hard, but putting it in is just as hard. The first time I had a group of men over to help. We got it in, but afterward there were a lot of complaints about sore backs.

The second set of bat houses that my wife begged me to put in went a little better. Instead of using my back, I used my brain!

I told my teenage son to get a bunch of his friends over and if they put in the pole, I would buy them pizza. My wallet was lighter, but my back didn't ache.

So before you start to build, think it all the way through, and follow the guidelines that I have mapped out for you, so you will have a bat house that will be enjoyed by all.

The Florida Keys

It is known that the lower keys in Florida have lots of mangroves, which produce and harbor many mosquitos. Richard Clyde Perky, a fishing lodge owner in Sugarloaf Key, dreamed of a developing a resort and wanted to control the mosquitos with a biological pest control method.

In 1929, he purchased plans for a bat tower from Charles Campbell of Texas. The tower was built for $10,000 and constructed 30ft tall with slats for roosting and a shoot for the bat guano. But after being built and bats being put in, they flew away and never returned.

It is believed that the reason why they left is due to no available fresh water. It has withstood many hurricanes, and is in good shape but still no bats—just a bird's nest on the top of the tower! There are three Campbell bat towers still standing out of the fourteen original worldwide. There are two in Texas and the one in Sugarloaf. A tower that was built in Temple Terrace, Florida was burned in 1979. It is now in the process of being rebuilt.

Bat houses that didn't work

The picture on page 25 is the bat house from Sugarloaf, Florida. This multi-chambered bat house built in 1929 by developer Richard Clyde Perky was a biological method to control mosquitos. Not realizing that bats need fresh water to survive which is in short supply in the Florida Keys he built it for naught. The bats after being put in left the first night and never returned.

A bat house in Lake Roger Park in Odessa, Florida was built in the woods right in amongst the trees not very high up off the ground. This was not a good place for the bats due to predators such as snakes. Bats also need to be able to drop from the house and fly off. With it being less than 6 feet off the ground they would have a very difficult time using their sonar to find their way before hitting the ground.

Another bat house built in Tampa, Florida is at Lopez Park. This one is far enough away from trees but is way too close to the ground for the bats to get the drop and fly away.

Bats can also be found sometimes under bridges. While on a bike ride in Clermont, Florida, I could smell the bat guano. It's a certain smell you will recognize right away!

Bats, Bats, Bats
How to Build a Bat House

Also, at the University of Florida, they have a very extensive bat facility. Visiting their web site is very helpful if you wish to learn more about bats.

I am an avid runner. One day while on a trail run, I ran up to a bat that was crawling on the ground. Looking closer, I noticed it was the same species as the bats that I have housed, Brazilian Free Tailed. I thought it might need assistance, but as I watched, it climbed up a pine tree. After climbing approximately 8 feet, it flew off on its own. Only later did I find out that bats cannot take off from the ground.

Occasionally a bat will fall out of its house. My wife came across one on the ground a few feet from the bat houses in the middle of the day. Not seeing any movement from the bat, she decided to bury it so our cats wouldn't "play" with it. With a shovel and gardening gloves she scooped it up. However, the bat was not dead and proceeded to flap its wings, but could not fly off. Thinking it needed assistance, she quickly scooped it up in her hands and propelled it into the air. The bat took off, made a circle, and swooped up into the bat house.

So, you see, if you find a bat on the ground, it may not be sick and dying. It may be looking for a higher perch to take off from.

Observations

If you look up on the Internet the instructions for building a bat house they will say, "DO NOT use pressure-treated wood or oil-based paint." At first, I followed these instructions and used untreated plywood and latex exterior paint. The reason they probably say that is the bats may eat the wood particles and chips of paint. Subsequently, due to moisture and mildew, the houses deteriorated within a few years.

I have since built four more houses with the more durable materials of pressure-treated wood and oil-based exterior paint.

There has been no drop off rate with my bat residents living in these new houses. All current bats have seemed healthy for years. Also on inspecting the bat houses periodically for maintenance, I have not seen any evidence of the bats eating the wood or paint.

Where My Story Ends . . .

After building my houses and mounting them, I waited. And I waited.

One month turned into six and my neighbors thought I had lost my mind. I built it like the specs said. *What could be wrong or missing?*

I knew if I left any pet food outside the raccoons and other critters would find that. *Why weren't the bats finding the brand-new condos I built just for them?*

Was it because they are blind? It is true they rely on sonar and have poor eyesight. It got me to thinking about fishermen at night on a lake, whipping their lines back and forth, and the bats flying near them. *Could it be the frequency of the whipping rods alerting them?*

Since I am a very poor fisherman, I didn't worry about stripping the reel from my fishing rod. That night at dusk, I whipped the rod through the air. I continued this for several months.

The neighbors thought I was crazy when I put up the poles but now watching me night after night whipping the fishing rod around the bat houses, they knew I was!

However, soon I noticed dark pellets at the base of the pole. No, I'm not kidding. It really did work.

The neighbors finally stopped kidding me about fishing in the back yard; because I really had caught some bats.

Oh, and by the way the neighbor's daughter that had the school project. . . Their house has no bats. Their bat house was just like mine, but they never did anything to attract any bats.

So, like any project you start, see it completely through. It really does have its own reward when you do!

What saying Goodbye to Mosquitos Meant

I currently have four bat houses mounted on 2 poles. Between the four houses, I have well over 200 bats.

Having these as nature's pest control means I can be outside at dusk. My wife and I can lie out on a blanket to watch a meteor shower.

I can also feel good about helping the environment by reducing the spreading of some diseases. You or I may help, if we have the right bats to fertilize plants because of the dwindling supply of bees.

The list of benefits of bat houses can go on and on, as more and more research is evolving from the study of bats. They are creatures that help our society, not a hindrance.

Bat Facts

There are over 1,000 species of bats. Bats are mammals; they make up about 25% of the mammal population, and are second-largest in population after the rodent. They can range in size from having a 5.9" wing span and weigh 0.09 oz. to the largest, with a 5'7" wingspan and weigh 4 lbs.

Bats do not flap their entire forelimbs as birds do, but flap their spread-out digits, which are long and covered with a thin membrane.

The blood-sucking bats that you hear about are mainly found in Mexico, and feed at night off cows. In zoos, they feed these types of bats by getting blood from butcher shops. Fruit bats and others make for great pollinators. With the epidemic of the bee pollinators dying off in mass amounts, we need bats to help any way they can.

They locate their food by using sonar, which is called Co-Echo Location.

Bats will consume between 3,000 and 5,000 insects in a night, depending on their size.

Bats can withstand a substantial amount of heat, which is why they need fresh water to rehydrate. At dusk when they leave their house, they will look for water first.

Bats, Bats, Bats
How to Build a Bat House

Bats live a very routine life. They sleep for 12 hours and hunt for 12 hours. They also have a pecking order. They live in the house in a hierarchy situation. The oldest and strongest are at the top. It's a lot cleaner up there, if you know what I mean.

Each night at dusk, they send out scouts to assess the situation, things like fresh water, food supply, rain, and temperature. The scouts report back and if conditions are good, the bats at the bottom will leave first. During breeding season, some bats will stay in the houses with the young, taking turns to hunt throughout the night.

They will hunt for about 12 hours and return at daybreak the next morning. At that time, you can see them flying around the bat house in loose circles waiting for their turn to go in. You may see one fly in, and immediately fly back out, and start circling until it's his turn to get his perch and all are snug in the house. And it is snug! We have looked in the house with a flashlight at dusk before they leave, and you can see they do not waste any space. They are packed in tight. Sometimes on a very hot Florida day, you can see a couple of bats hanging from the bottom of the screen below the lower vent, or on the outside hanging on the pole, due to the heat that builds up in the houses.

When it gets cold in Florida, they will find a warmer place to stay. I am not sure where they go, but when the weather gets a little warmer, they come right back.

In July and August, they have their babies and there are always a couple of bats that stay with the babies in the houses.

A fun thing to do is, at dusk go out and watch the bats leave for the night. It is very interesting to watch them fall out and take off. We have learned not to stand too close to the houses, due to them falling out so fast. Not because they will fly into you (we have never had a bat do this), but that it is a little unnerving to have so many fly down at once and swerve around you as they fly away.

Stand back and count how many bats you have. You will be amazed at how many are in the house.

About the Author

I'm a builder and a fixer. I have had people give me things that aren't working and say, *fix it and it's yours*. This problem of the mosquitos was something that was keeping me from enjoying my own yard. I couldn't let that happen. I had to fix my problem. It might not be 100%, but it's a start.

I'm also a person that believes we should take care of the planet that we live on. To that end, we recycle and use reusable bags at the store. We have a garden and our own compost. The effects of using chemicals on plants is not a good thing for our bodies or our ground water.

Whether you believe in climate change or not, it has been proven that we are poisoning our water supply with chemicals and debris in the water. We have been having record warm months. The mosquitos have longer breeding times when we have less cool weather. This warmer weather will bring in more disease threats. I cannot see how using biological pest control is not worth a try if you have the right conditions to maintain bats in your area.

Some Valuable Resources

www.floridabats.org

www.flmnh.ufl.edu/bats

http://www.bats.org.uk/pages/all_about_bats.html

These links are being provided as a convenience and for informational purposes only; they do not constitute an endorsement or an approval by the publisher or the author of any of the products, services or opinions on the third party website. Neither JoHazel Publishing nor author (s) bears no responsibility for the accuracy, legality or content of the external sites or for that of subsequent links. Contact the external site for answers to questions regarding its content.

Thank you for reading.

JoHazel Publishing

Please visit our website, where you can browse our book and author listings. Non-fictional books will be listed in our Knowledge series.
We offer a wide selection of novels and novellas in different genres for our fiction readers.

www.johazelpublishing.com

Notes:

Notes:

Made in the USA
San Bernardino, CA
10 August 2019